The Tale of Fall Landon Sully
The Pirate Cat

Volume 1

Written by: Erik Larson

Chapter One

In the Beginning...

Far, far out into the ocean sailed two brother bandits. The older brother, named Bobby, was the most skilled thief of all the lands. There was nothing he couldn't steal without you knowing. And always by his side was his little brother, Billy. Billy was his faithful accomplice. A little clumsy at times but always there when he needed him. One day, while sailing on the deep blue sea, Bobby noticed they were running low on supplies. So they decided to dock in a nearby harbor of a small coastal village. The bandits decided they would rob the villagers that night once the sun had set and darkness had fallen. With a few hours left until nightfall, the two bandits sat back in their boat, closed their eyes and took a nap. After a restful couple of hours, evening came and soon followed the dark night sky, lit only by the twinkling of little stars shinning above. Now was the time to get going on their night of mischief. So off they headed, sneaking through the village streets and making a stop at each and every house. The bandits were stealing all the treasure they could get their hands on.

"This should be enough," said Bobby, barely able to carry his burlap sack, which was over flowing with jewels and treasures.

"I think so too," said Billy. "I'm pretty much all out of room and all I have left is a small burlap bag which can't hold much anyway," he continued.

"Well then, I say it's time for us to head back to our boat," said Bobby.

"You got it," said Billy.

So through the dark ally they crept, tip toeing silently as to not wake any of the villagers. They had almost reached the harbor when suddenly they heard loud meowing coming from one of the houses just up ahead. A little cat had spotted them!

"Oh no!" said Bobby worriedly. "If that cat keeps meowing the whole street will wake up and see that we have stolen all their treasure!"

"What should we do then?" asked Billy.

"I know! You said you had one small burlap bag left that was still empty, right?" asked Bobby.

"I sure do Bobby. But how will that help us?" asked Billy.

"Just follow me," said Bobby.
Bobby snatched the burlap bag from Billy's belt loop and shook it open.

Bobby went on to explain his plan to Billy. "Now, when we get close enough to the cat, I want you to reach down like you are going to pet it and then grab the cat and throw it into the sack," boasted Bobby.

"Wow, Bobby! That is sure to work! What a great plan!" said Billy.

As the bandits walked closer to the house, the meowing grew louder and louder. Billy looked at Bobby. With one nod of Bobby's head Billy walked up to the little cat and reached out like he was going to pet him.

"Here kitty, kitty, kitty. Come on. I have something for you," Billy whispered to the little cat. Curiosity got the best of the little cat. So off he went, walking straight up to Billy, purring loudly.

"Gotcha, you little rascal!" Billy said excitedly, grabbing hold of the cat's scruff.

"Good job, Billy. Now hurry up and toss him into the sack," said Bobby.

And with that, the little cat was dropped into the burlap sack and Bobby pulled the cinch tight.

"Now we have to hurry up and get out of here before the sun rises and the villagers wake up," said Bobby.

Billy agreed. So off they crept following the tiny road that lead to the dock in the harbor where their sailboat was moored.

"Billy, when we get to the boat I want you to load up all our treasures and supplies while I get the boat ready to set sail," ordered Bobby.

"No problem Bobby," said Billy. "I can handle that."

Upon arriving at their sailboat each bandit started on their own task at hand. Billy began loading up all the satchels and supplies while Bobby checked the sails and ropes to make sure everything was in good sailing condition. With each bandit finished with their tasks, they were now ready to set sail. And just in time too, as the sun was just about to rise.

"Now, are you sure everything is loaded on the boat?" asked Bobby.

"Oh darn! I forgot the satchel with that little cat in it," said Billy.

Jumping off the sailboat and onto the dock, Billy ran over and grabbed the small satchel that held the little cat inside. Billy headed back towards the boat and hopped into it. With everything now loaded onboard they were ready to set sail.

"Okay Bobby. Now everything is loaded on the boat. We are good to go!" exclaimed Billy.

With one last cast off of the ropes, the sailboat was heading out of the harbor and into the vast deep blue sea.

"Ha, ha, ha" laughed Bobby. "That was almost too easy."

"Well, how are you going to do that?" asked Windy.

Fall thought for a second. "Well first I am going to try and pry the lock open with my paws," he said. So Fall grabbed the heavy metal lock in his paws and pulled with all his might. But nothing happened. The lock was just too strong.

"So now how are you going to get out?" asked Windy.

"I will have to pick the lock open…with one of these sticks," said Fall.

With that said, he picked up a loose stick from the floor of his cage and tried to pick the metal lock. Snap! His wooden stick broke into pieces and the lock was still locked tight.

"Uh oh," said Windy. "Now what will you do?"

"I'll…I'll just…" Tears began fill Fall's eyes. "I will get out of here. I just have to. I can't be locked up like this. I didn't do anything wrong!" cried Fall.

"Please, Fall, don't cry. I will help you figure out a way to get out of that cage," said Windy.

"But how, Windy? You are not able to come onto land. You have to stay in the ocean in order to live. How will you help me?" asked Fall.

Windy knew what Fall said was right. *How can I help him if I can't even go onto land and help him break out of that cage?* thought Windy. Just then she thought about her best friend, Mia the mermaid.

"I know," Windy exclaimed. "I will go get Mia to help us. She is a mermaid and very clever. She knows a lot about human things like that cage and even that lock. She will surely know what to do!"

"Do you think she will really come to help me?" asked Fall.

"Of course. We are best friends and we help each other out all the time. I will be back, Fall. And don't you worry! We'll get you out of that horrible cage. I promise."

And with a splash, Windy disappeared under the sea. After a couple of hours, Fall began to feel very lonely. There was no one to talk to and no one to play with. He started thinking about all the fun times he had back home, running around in the grassy fields, snuggling up in his favorite basket and laying out on the warm sandy beach. Oh how he missed being free. But all Fall could do now was huddle down in the back of his wooden cage, close his eyes and hope that tomorrow would be a better day. And with that thought, Fall fell into a deep peaceful sleep.

Chapter Two

Finding Help…

Through the ocean, Windy swam as fast as her tail could push her. "Oh, where is Mia," she said. "Oh, I know. She is usually sunbathing about this time. Yes, I will go to Turtle Island to see if I can catch her there." So away she swam as fast as she could.

It wasn't long until Windy arrived at Turtle Island. It was warm and sunny out so she knew Mia had to be there on the beach. Windy looked up and down the beach. No Mia. She swam to the other side of the island to check the beach there. Mia was nowhere in sight. *What do I do now?* Windy thought. *I just have to find Mia. That is the only way I can help Fall get out of that horrible cage.*

Just as Windy turned to dive down into the sea, up splashed Mia right next to her.

"Oh Mia!" exclaimed Windy. "I am so happy to see you!"

"What are you doing all the way out here? And by yourself?" asked Mia.

"I need your help…there is this little cat…locked in a cage…no way out…no food or water…please Mia you must help me" exclaimed Windy.

"Oh my! How can that be? Someone really locked a little cat in a cage? How awful! Of course I will help you, Windy. You just lead the way!" said Mia.

And away Windy and Mia went. Swimming full speed all the way back to Smugglers Isle and the secret island hideout where Fall was being held captive.

"Psss…Psss…Fall. Wake up, Fall," said Windy.

Fall slowly opened his eyes and stretched out his paws with a big yawn. Still a little groggy from his nap, he tried to focus his eyes down on the seashore. He could see Windy there but who was that next to her? *Was that Mia the mermaid that Windy told him about? Did she really come all the way out here to help rescue him?* Fall thought.

"Hey Fall. Look! I told you I would get Mia to help you. We will get you out of that cage now for sure!" said Windy excitedly.

"Oh you poor little guy," Mia said to Fall. "Are you alright?"

"I'm okay," Fall said. "But I am getting pretty thirsty and hungry. I can hear my tummy growling."

"You just hang in there, Fall. We will get you out of that cage one way or another. Don't you worry," said Mia.

Mia turned to look at the horizon. The sun was close to setting. Knowing that once the sun had set and darkness had fallen, it would be impossible to see what she was doing. She had to work fast. *But how was she going to get that cage open?* Mia thought. She looked around the seashore for any ideas on how to possibly do this. And then her eyes fell upon a long, strong looking branch on the beach. Mia had an idea! She swam over to the shoreline and reached out to grab the stick. With her hands, she removed all the little branches until it was just a nice sturdy pole. She turned and swam back to Fall.

"Okay, Fall. First, I am going to try and knock the lock with this pole. It is good and strong so it might just break that lock. Then you can remove the lock with your paws," Mia explained. "So move to the back of the cage, close your eyes and cover your head."

Fall listened to Mia and immediately moved to the back of the cage, closing his eyes and covering his head.

"Are you ready?" asked Mia.

"Yes," said Fall.

"Okay, here it goes," said Mia.

Mia grabbed ahold tightly to the pole and swung it as hard as she could against the big metal lock. Clunk! The cage went swinging from side to side. But the lock didn't budge one bit. Mia's heart dropped. The lock was stronger than she expected. But there was no way she was going to give up.

"Hold on Fall, I am going to try it one more time," said Mia.

With his eyes still shut and paws covering his head, Fall replied, "Okay. Go for it, Mia!"

Fall braced himself for the next blow. Mia grabbed ahold of the pole again and swung it with all her might. Clunk! The cage looked as if it might swing right off the tree. But still, the lock didn't break.

"Oh no," said Windy. "It didn't work."

Fall opened his eyes and saw that the metal lock was still there. He moved to the front of the cage and grabbed it with this paws. Pulling as hard as he could, he tried to pry the lock open. But it didn't budge. Fall pulled again with all his strength until all the energy left his body. His paws dropped from the lock and he fell to the cage floor. He looked up at the cage door and the heavy lock was still there.

"Fall, are you okay?" asked Windy.

"I'm okay Windy," Fall sighed. "Do you have any other ideas, Mia? I just have to get out of this cage. I just have to!" cried Fall.

Mia was lost in her thoughts. Feeling terrible that she couldn't break the lock off the cage, she had to come up with another idea. Thinking as hard as she could, Mia swam the shoreline to see if any ideas would come to her. And then she got one.

"I got it!" Mia said. "We'll try to pull the cage door off with a rope of seaweed. Since we can't break the lock or pry it open we have to try the get the whole cage door off."

Mia turned around and dove under the water, searching for the perfect seaweed to braid into a rope. The perfect seaweed had to be long and strong for what she needed it to do. After a few minutes of searching she had found it. Grabbing a handful she swam back up to the surface.

"I got it. I found the seaweed!" exclaimed Mia. "Now all I have to do is braid it into a long and sturdy rope."

Mia turned back to the horizon again. The sun had begun to set. She didn't have much time left. She quickly began braiding the seaweed together to make a long and strong rope. A few minutes had passed and then she was finished. The rope was the perfect length and seemed to be very strong indeed.

"This should do it," said Mia, as she lifted the rope out of the water. "Now Fall, I am going to throw one end over to you and you need to tie it tightly onto the cage door. Can you do that?"

"Yes Mia," said Fall.

Mia flung one end of the rope out towards Fall. He put his paws out through the wooden bars and caught the end of the rope. Grabbing ahold of it tightly, Fall started to pull in some more rope to get it around the cage door. Once he had it wrapped around the cage door and tied tightly, he gave it a final tug to make sure it would not slip off.

"Okay Mia. I am ready when you are!" exclaimed Fall.

"Now I need you to do the same thing as before Fall. Get to the back of the cage and cover your head," said Mia.

Fall listened to Mia's directions and did exactly what she said.

"I'm ready!" said Fall.

Mia turned to Windy, "I need your help, Windy. You have to grab ahold of the rope with me and when I say pull, we both have to swim and pull as hard as we can to try and get that door off. Can you help me?" asked Mia.

"Of course I can!" said Windy.

"Okay! Are you ready?" asked Mia.

"Ready!" said Windy.

"Pull!" exclaimed Mia.

Both Windy and Mia shot through the water as fast and as hard as they could. The rope pulled tight and they both pulled and pulled with all their might. But the cage door wasn't moving. No matter how hard they pulled, the cage door just didn't budge.

"Again! Pull again!" exclaimed Mia.

So again, Windy and Mia pulled with all their might. Putting every last bit of their energy into pulling the seaweed rope. Exhausted from using up all their strength, both of them let go of the rope. Catching their breath, they looked up at the cage door. It was still in place, as if nothing ever happened. Fall slowly opened his eyes. Everything was exactly the same. The cage door was just too strong to be broken open. Warm tears began to fall from Fall's eyes. Quickly wiping them away, he put on a brave face.

"Thanks for trying, both of you. I really mean that too! Even though it didn't work out it must have been really hard on you both. It is getting dark now and we won't be able to see much once night falls," Fall said to Mia and Windy.

"Oh Fall, I am so sorry," said Mia.

"Me too Fall," said Windy.

"There is nothing to be sorry about," said Fall. "You both tried your best to help me get out of this cage and that means a lot to me. You should be getting home now since it's getting dark. Your families must be worried about you."

Fall slowly turned round and headed to the back of his cage. His tummy was growling from hunger and he was very thirsty. He laid his head down on his paws and closed his eyes. Just then Mia had a great idea!

"I got it! I can get Caden the pirate to help us! I don't know why I didn't think of this before. There is no other man on the whole sea that is stronger or more clever than him. Plus, Caden is a human! He can go onto shore and get you out of that cage!" Mia could hardly contain her excitement.

"That is a great idea, Mia!" said Windy. "With Caden being a human, he is sure to be able to get Fall freed from that cage!"

Fall opened his eyes and asked, "Who is Caden?"

"He is the strongest, bravest, most handsome pirate of all the seas. He always helps others in need and it doesn't matter what it takes, he will do it. People everywhere call him The Pirate with a Heart of Gold," sighed Mia, with a bashful smile.

Fall suddenly remembered hearing stories about The Pirate with a Heart of Gold from sailors down on the docks in his old hometown. *Was this the same pirate that Mia was talking about? The pirate who fought for justice on the high seas? Who never turned away someone in need of his help? If so, this cage didn't stand a chance against him.* Fall felt hopeful again.

"Wow Fall! Caden is surely the one who can get you out of that cage. He is so strong that there isn't a cage he can't get into or a lock he couldn't break," said Windy.

With the darkness of nightfall moments away, Mia knew that there was nothing else they could do for now. So she decided to start making her way out to sea to find Caden.

"Okay you two," said Mia. "I am going to set out to find Caden and bring him back here to help with the rescue of Fall.

Windy, can you stay here for a little while longer to make sure Fall's all right?"

"Of course I can," said Windy.

"Fall, no matter what it takes, I will bring Caden back here to rescue you. Will you be okay?" asked Mia.

Fall stood up tall and put a big smile on his face, "Of course I will be okay. I am lucky to have found such caring friends as you both."

Mia turned to Windy, "Now you keep an eye out for any trouble and make sure Fall is alright."

"Oh yes Mia. Of course I will. You can count on me!" smiled Windy.

With a wink of her eye and a splash of her tail, Mia turned towards the open sea and disappeared into the darkness of night.

"Wow, I can't believe that Caden the pirate will come to rescue me. I have only heard tales of him. Of his bravery, honor and strength. I can't wait to meet him!" Fall said excitedly.

" Oh, yes, Fall. Caden is a wonderful pirate. And he is so very handsome, too." Windy said with blushing cheeks.

"How do you know Caden?" asked Fall.

"Caden helped my family out once when we were in trouble too. My dad and I were out in a cove one day and he got caught up in a fishing net. The more my dad struggled to get free the tighter the net became, so I rushed to Mia for help. Mia raced out and brought back Caden. He cut the fishing net loose and freed my dad. Ever since then my dad has been going with Caden on all his voyages, protecting his ship from any dangers. They travel everywhere together," explained Windy.

"Caden sounds like a really cool pirate," said Fall. "I can't wait to meet him and your dad too!"

Windy smiled and thought to herself that she would like to see Caden and her dad again too! Shinning stars, high up in the sky, broke the darkness of the night and sparkled down on the water like little white jewels. Windy thought about how her mom must be worried about her not being home yet.

"I think I better be heading home for the night Fall," said Windy. "Will you be okay until tomorrow morning?"

"Yes Windy. You better get going so your mom doesn't worry too much about you being out after dark. I'll be fine. Don't you worry about me," said Fall, smiling.

"I'm really sorry to leave you Fall, but I will be back first thing in the morning," said Windy.

"Okay. See you tomorrow morning then. And be safe on your way home!" said Fall.

A moment later Windy was gone, having dove under the water and making her way home. Fall looked up at the sky. All the twinkling stars looked so pretty. Shining through the darkness across the night sky went a shooting star. Fall closed his eyes and made a wish. *I wish Caden the pirate comes back with Mia tomorrow and frees me from this cage.* Fall wished upon that star as hard as he could. Now only time could tell if his wish would come true.

Settling down in his cage for the night, Fall could hear his tummy growling. He was so very hungry and thirsty. And the bandits hadn't been back to check on him since they arrived earlier today. But he couldn't think about it. If he did, it just made it worse. So he curled up in the back of his cage and closed his eyes, thinking about tomorrow and meeting Caden!

Just as Fall was about to fall into a deep sleep, he heard a rustling in the trees behind him. Startled, he jumped to his feet and looked around outside of his cage. Trying to peer though the darkness of night, Fall could just make out a shadow of something in the trees. It was moving from tree to tree and branch to branch. Suddenly the shadow landed on top of Fall's cage. He could see it clearly now. It was a young monkey!

"Here you go," said the young monkey reaching out his hands showing Fall a banana and tiny melon.

"Is this for me?" asked Fall.

"Of course it is. I thought you might be hungry," said the young monkey.

Fall slowly reached his paws out and took the food from the monkey.

"Thank you," said Fall. "My stomach was beginning to hurt I was so hungry. I haven't had anything to eat in quite some time."

Fall was so hungry he couldn't stand to wait any longer. He peeled back the skin of the banana and took a great big bite. Fall couldn't remember ever having a banana that tasted this good. He wasn't sure if it was because he was so hungry or if it was because it was grown on this island. Either way, he was happy to have something to put in his belly.

"Don't you get scared out here at night all by yourself?" asked Fall with banana still in his mouth.

"Nah," said the young monkey. "My parents are close by and plus all the animals here look out for one another. That is how we heard about you. Everyone was talking about how you were locked up here without any food or water. So I volunteered to come here tonight to give you the food! But I wanted to wait until nightfall to visit you to be sure I wouldn't run into those bandits."

"Wow, this sure is a cool place. Everyone has been so nice and friendly to me. Thank you for coming by to see me and thanks again for the food," said Fall.

"Well, I better be getting back now," said the young monkey. "My mom hates it when I stay away from home too long at night. Maybe I'll see you around when you get out of that cage."

The young monkey turned around, sprung off the top of the cage and into a nearby tree. Before Fall could say goodbye, the young monkey had already disappeared into the trees. Fall just smiled and looked down at the melon he had left. He was still a bit hungry. Fall picked up the melon and hit it against one of the wooden bars of his cage. Crack! The melon split into two pieces. Fall sat down and finished off the sweet, juicy melon. With his tummy full and a smile on his face, Fall settled down in the back of his cage to rest for the night. Yawning happily, he closed his eyes and fell fast asleep.

Chapter Three

Weathering the Storm...

    Out on the open sea sailed Caden the pirate. And by his side was his faithful companion Gussy, the parrot and Fin, Windy's dad. Standing at the helm of the ship, Caden noticed a shadow in the water up ahead. It seems to be moving at lightning speed towards his ship.

    "Well what do you think that could be, Gussy?" asked Caden. "Looks too small to be a whale or a shark. And too big to be any fish around this part of the sea."

    "Ah, don't worry about it Caden," said Gussy. "Fin will take care of it. He is the best ship guard out here. No one can get near us with him guarding our ship."

    As the shadow got closer Fin moved in to block its path. To his amazement he recognized the shadow. It was Mia. *But what was she doing way out here and in such a hurry as well?* Fin thought.

    "Whoa, whoa, whoa, Mia. Slow down," said Fin. "You could get yourself hurt swimming that fast if you don't pay proper attention. What's all the fuss about?"

    "Oh Fin, I am so happy I found you guys. I need to speak with Caden right away. I have been swimming all night to get here. I really need his help with something!" exclaimed Mia.

    "Okay, okay. Calm down. You can go right up to the ship and see Caden," said Fin.

    Mia swam right up next to the ship and splashed to the surface. Trying to catch her breath she called out to Caden.

    "Caden! Gussy! I need your help! Where are you two?" asked Mia.

Caden and Gussy appeared from over the ship's railing. Then Fin popped up to the surface.

"What's wrong Mia?" asked Caden.

Mia went into the whole story about Fall. How the bandit brothers had captured him in his hometown so they wouldn't be caught after they robbed all the villagers. And now how he was being held captive on Smugglers Isle at their secret hideout. She told them how sad and lonely Fall was but how he kept hope of being freed from that cage. As Mia went on explaining the story, Caden looked out over the sea, feeling a tugging at his heart and then feeling the blood boil in his veins. Above anything else, Caden disliked people who were cruel to animals. There was no reason to mistreat an innocent animal. Caden pictured Fall, sitting all alone in that wooden cage, hungry and thirsty, with no one taking care of him. Furious at that image, he shook his head and turned towards Mia.

"Of course I will help you Mia. It seems like there is no time to waste. So please, you lead the way. We will head to Fall at once!" stated Caden.

Mia turned around and looked back in the direction she just came from. Dark grey clouds were filling the horizon and loud thunder rolled across the sea. This was a sure sign of a storm brewing and right in the middle of their path to rescue Fall. The winds were picking up and the sea began to rise and fall.

"We need to head in that direction," said Mia, pointing straight into the storm. "That is the quickest way to Smugglers Isle."

Caden looked into the horizon. Scanning the darkness of the clouds and the drastic rise and fall of the sea, he knew all too well that these types of storms were the worst. Lightning cracked down and lit up the darkening sky. Huge, cold raindrops began to fall.

The wind was so strong now Gussy was having a hard time hanging onto the ship's railing.

"You better go down below Gussy," said Caden. "It looks like this is going to be one vicious storm."

"You don't have to tell me twice," said Gussy as he made his way down below deck.

Even with knowing it was dangerous to sail through such a strong storm, Caden had no hesitation to go and rescue Fall.

"Don't worry Caden," said Fin. "I will help guide you through that storm. You can count on me!"

"Alright everybody! We are heading out!" shouted Caden over the thunder. He turned around and walked over to his bulk box where he kept his ship's gear and, most importantly, his pirate flag. He grabbed the black and red flag, walked over to the flagpole and hoisted it up. The flag flapped wildly in the wind. Now they were ready to sail through the storm. Their voyage had officially begun.

Mia was fighting hard to swim as fast as she could. The strong currents were pushing against her making it twice as hard to swim. She quickly began to get tired. Just then, Fin came up behind her and took her on his fin.

"Here Mia. Just hang on and guide me in the right direction. I will get us through this storm," said Fin.

"Thanks Fin. I know I can count on you to do your best," said Mia.

Mia held on tight to Fin's dorsal fin and away they went, plowing through the rough currents and heading towards the secret hideout.

The storm seemed to last forever. At least it felt like forever. Then finally, as quickly as the storm had arrived, it had passed. Leaving behind a beautiful pink and red sky. The once high seas leveled out to a flat glassy surface. Gussy popped his head up from the hatch.

"Is it safe to come out now?" asked Gussy.

"Yes Gussy," Caden said walking over to the hatch. "You can come out now."

With a single leap for take off, Gussy flew into the fresh air, stretching his wings.

"Ah this feels great. There is nothing better than flying around in the crisp air just after a storm," said Gussy.

Caden looked around for Fin and Mia. But they were nowhere to be seen. He did a full walk around the ship, looking over the railing into the water to see if he could locate them, but still nothing. No sight of them anywhere.

"That's strange," Caden said scratching his head. "They were in front of the ship just a little while ago. Hum…I hope they are all right."

Just then he heard a splash! Up came Fin with Mia to the surface. Looking exhausted but happy to see that the storm had passed.

"Whew. I am glad to see you both are okay. I was worried there for a second," said Caden.

"Of course we are okay and it is all thanks to Fin," Mia said giving Fin a hug. "I was getting so tired swimming against the rough currents and then Fin swooped in and helped me. He is such a great whale and a great swimmer, too!"

"Ah, thanks Mia," blushed Fin. "We better get going now. We still have a long way to go until we reach Fall."

With no more time to waste, off they went. Making their way back towards the bandit's secret hideout. With each one of them anxious to get there as fast as they could, everyone was moving at full speed ahead.

Earlier, back at Smugglers Isle, morning had come and as promised, Windy returned.

"Good morning Fall!" said Windy excitedly. But no reply came. "Fall…Fall? Are you awake?" asked Windy.

Fall rolled over and slowly opened his eyes. Rising to his feet and stretching he replied, "Yes Windy. I am awake."

"Oh good. Well today is the day Fall! The day you get freed from that cage! Aren't you excited?" asked Windy.

Fall just then remembered that today he was going to meet Caden, the most famous pirate of them all. "Oh you're right Windy. I get to meet Caden today!" he said excitedly.

Windy splashed around happily and Fall pounced around in his cage smiling and laughing. He couldn't stop thinking about what Caden would look like or how he would talk. How big his ship was and what kind of treasures he would have onboard. There was so much Fall wanted to know about Caden. He just couldn't wait to meet him!

But just then Windy felt the temperature of the ocean water around her drop. And she knew what that meant. It meant a storm was coming. A strong storm too. Windy spun around to look at the horizon and, just as she had thought, a storm was coming. Large dark clouds were filling the sky and covering the sun. Thick mist rolled on the surface of the sea, heading right towards them.

"Oh no Fall," said Windy. "This is not good. Not good at all."

"What's wrong Windy?" asked Fall, seeing the worried expression on her face.

"There is a really big storm heading right our way!" exclaimed Windy.

A moment later, large cold raindrops began to fall from the sky. A strong gust of wind ripped through the cove shaking all the trees and loud thunder rolled across the sky. The thick mist had reached the cove, making it impossible to see anything. Poor Fall, with no shelter from the wind and rain he just huddled in the back of his cage. A loud crack of lightning lit up the sky and Fall covered his ears, trembling with fear.

The sea began to rise and fall with large waves crashing onto the beach. Windy was having a hard time keeping herself steadily afloat. With the seas rising and falling and the wind whipping around her, she had no other choice except to submerge under the water to safety.

Fall thought the storm was never going to end. The large cold raindrops just kept falling on him. Soaking through his fur right down to his skin. He was so cold he began to shiver. The tall thin coconut trees swayed in the wind and coconuts were being thrown through the air. The beautiful tropical flowers that were blooming on the beaches edge were now being torn into pieces from the strong wind. Leaves and sticks were flying all over the place. *Why is this happening to me?* Fall thought. Fall began to feel very sad and scared. He couldn't stop the tears from falling from his eyes. His poor paws were frozen from trying to protect himself from the cold rain. With no way to escape the rain and wind, he just had to lie there and wait out the storm. *But how much longer would it last?*

And with that thought, the rain began to stop. The thick mist slowly disappeared and the dark grey clouds began to fade away. Fall opened his eyes. He looked up at the pink and orange sky left in the aftermath of the storm. The sun began to peak through the clouds until it was shining at its full brightness. The storm had passed! Fall had survived. He wiped the last tear away with his paw and smiled into the sun, feeling the warm tingling of the sun's rays on his face.

Just then, up popped Windy to the surface of the water. With rosy cheeks she bashfully smiled at Fall.

"I'm sorry for leaving you all alone Fall," she said. "I just couldn't stay steady on the surface of the water any longer. It was just too rough for me," Windy explained. "I hope you are not mad at me Fall."

"Mad at you? Oh Windy, I could never be mad at you. You did the right thing by protecting yourself. You have been such a great friend to me that I don't know what I would have done if something bad had happened to you," said Fall.

Fall looked out into the horizon of the sea. It was so calm and peaceful now that it was hard to imagine, just moments ago, a vicious storm had passed through here. Now all they had to do was wait for Mia and Caden to arrive and then finally Fall would be freed from that horrible wooden cage.

Chapter Four

Caden to the Rescue ...

Several hours had gone by since the storm had passed and Fall and Windy were getting a bit nervous that they hadn't seen Mia or Caden yet. Windy was especially worried since she knew her dad would have been with them guarding Caden's ship. Just then something caught Fall's eyes. It looked like something was splashing in and out of the water, coming closer and closer, heading towards the shore.

"What could that be?" asked Fall. "It's a tail! Yes! A tail! Look Windy! Mia is heading straight towards us. But where are Caden and his pirate ship? There is no one behind her!"

Mia reached the shore with a big splash.

"Oh Mia!" exclaimed Windy. "I am so glad you are alright.

"Me too!" said Fall.

"You guys...did you think a little storm like that would keep me from helping rescue Fall?" Mia smiled and turned towards Fall. "And look Fall. Look who I brought back with me."

Mia spun around and pointed in the direction of the horizon, expecting Caden's pirate ship to be sailing towards them. But there was no ship in sight.

Mia gasped, "Oh no! Where are they? I thought they were right behind me."

Windy's eyes widened with fear and she asked, "Mia...was my dad guarding Caden's ship?"

Mia's heart sank. "Oh, Windy. I am so sorry. What have I done?" Mia began to cry, her tears falling into the salty seawater. Everyone was very quiet. Tears began to well up in Windy's eyes and Fall just hung his head in sorrow. He knew he would never get out of his cage now. And now, because of him, Caden and Windy's dad might be in trouble, or even worse, lost at sea.

Just then, little bubbles rose to the surface of the water. A few at first, and then more, and more, and even more. The bubbles grew larger and larger until finally up popped Fin. Windy could hardly believe her eyes!

"Daddy! You are all right! I was so worried about you. I thought something awful had happened to you!" exclaimed Windy.

"Of course I am all right, sweetheart. I will always be here for you," and Fin leaned over and gave Windy a little kiss on the top of her head.

Fall raised his head in excitement and was so happy to see that Fin had made it to shore safely. And just then he saw it! Caden's pirate ship.

"Look! Look out there!" exclaimed Fall. "It's a pirate ship isn't it?"

Everyone turned towards the sea's horizon and saw a ship heading their way. It was Caden's pirate ship all right. As the ship got closer they could see Gussy flying in front of the bow. He swooped down and landed on the white sandy beach right near Fall's cage.

"Gussy! Boy, are you a sight for sore eyes!" said Mia. "I am so happy you guys made it here safe and sound."

"The wind died down for a little bit so it was slow sailing at times. That is why we are a little late getting here," explained Gussy.

"I'm just so happy you made it. I was so worried, but now seeing that you are both okay, I feel much better," said Mia. "I am going to swim out to meet Caden." With that said, Mia spun around and dove under the water.

Once his ship was safely inside the cove, Caden dropped anchor. After he lowered the dinghy into the water, Caden grabbed a set of paddles and climbed down into it. As soon as he began rowing, Mia sprang up from the water right next to his dinghy.

"Hey Caden! I am glad to see you are all right," Mia said with a big smile on her face. "But I did begin to worry when I got here and noticed that guys weren't behind me."

"Oh Mia, you worry too much!" said Caden. "But thank you for your concern. Wow, looks like the whole gang is already here."

"We were all just waiting for you!" exclaimed Mia. "Shall I lead the way?"

"Of course," said Caden.

So Mia lead the way back towards the shore, everyone watching them as they approached the beach. Caden reached the white sandy beach and jumped out of the dinghy. His eyes immediately fell upon Fall. His soft white fur was soaking wet with bits of leaves and twigs stuck all over him. Caden could feel that tugging at his heart again. He just couldn't believe what he was seeing. What a horrible thing to do to such a cute little cat. Caden walked right up to Fall's cage.

"You poor little fella. Are you all right?" he asked Fall.

Fall couldn't believe his eyes. He stepped closer to the front of his cage and peered up at Caden with his big blue sparkling eyes. Fall couldn't help but purr. And purr he did, as loud as he could.

"Wow, I can't believe you are really here," said Fall. "I have heard so many tales about you and all the good deeds you do. Oh, and yes, I am all right. Especially now that you are here!" exclaimed Fall.

"Mia told me everything about you. How you were taken from your home and locked up in this horrible cage. You must have been so frightened," said Caden.

Fall's bottom lip quivered and he shed a single tear.

"Why are you crying little one? Are you hurt somewhere?" asked Caden.

"No...I'm fine," said Fall. "It's just that I'm so happy you are here. That someone has cared enough to come all this way to help me."

Caden reached his hands through the wooden bars and scratched Fall's on his head.

"What do you say we get you out of this cage now?" asked Caden.

"Oh yes please," said Fall.

"Okay. Now Fall, I need you to back away from the front of the cage, close your eyes and cover your head with your paws. I am going to break this lock off the door to get you out of there," explained Caden.

Fall quickly moved the to the back of his cage as far away from the door as possible. Caden reached down and unsheathed his sword.

"Whoa," said Fall. "So that's what a real pirate sword looks like!"

"Okay Fall, I need you to cover your head with your paws now and close your eyes," Caden said.

Fall followed Caden's orders. He put his paws on his head and closed his eyes tight. Caden then counted down from three and...whack! With one swift swing of his sword the lock was cut into two. The dark metal lock fell upon the white sand below and the wooden door of the cage swung open. Fall slowly opened his eyes. In amazement he just gazed at the open cage door.

"You did it!" cried Fall. "You really did it, Caden! I can't believe it. You broke the lock!"

Windy and Mia swam around excitedly. Gussy began to whistle and flapped his wings. Fin blew water from his blowhole, creating a magical looking fountain. Everyone was so happy and excited.

Caden slid his sword back into his sheath and looked over at Fall. With a warm smile, he reached out his hands. Fall stepped to the front of his cage and in a single bound leapt into Caden's arms. Finally, Fall's dream of being free again had come true. And it was all thanks to his new friends. He felt like the luckiest cat in the whole world!

Just then a loud rustling came from the bushes behind them. Everyone stopped and became very still.

"Well, well, well," said a familiar voice. "What do we have here?"

Coming out of the bushes were the two brother bandits, holding large wooden clubs in their hands.

"Looks like someone is trying to steal what belongs to us," said Billy the bandit.

"It sure does, Billy. And robbing us in broad daylight too!" exclaimed Bobby the bandit. "Not only are you trying to steal from me but this is my land and you are trespassing on it as well!"

"Yeah…and if you know what is good for you, you will put that cat back in the cage and get off our island," added Billy. Caden looked Bobby straight in the eyes.

"So…you must be the two bandits that I have heard so much about," said Caden. "Stealing from hard working people and causing mischief and mayhem wherever you go. But on your last trip you did something that brought me all the way here."

"Oh yeah, and what was that?" asked Bobby the bandit.

"You captured and caged an innocent little cat for no other reason than to save your own skin. And using an animal like that is not going to slide with me," said Caden.

The two bandits stepped in closer towards Caden. Caden turned and handed Fall over to Mia.

"Keep him safe for me for a little while," he told Mia.

Mia nodded her head and cradled Fall in her arms. Swimming away from the shore she was careful to keep Fall above the water and not get him wet. Caden turned back towards the bandits.

"And just who do you think you are telling us about right and wrong, Mr. Pirate!" exclaimed Bobby the bandit. "The way I see it, you are no better than us. All you pirates are the same. Robbing and frightening people everywhere you go. So what gives you the right to put us down?"

"Yeah," said Billy the bandit. "Pirates are just as bad as bandits and thieves."

Caden took a step closer to the bandits. Looking Bobby straight in the eyes he said, "Do you even know who I am?"

Bobby turned to Billy. They both shrugged their shoulders. Neither of them knew who he was but there was something familiar about his face. However, they couldn't quite figure out where they had seen him before.

"Nope," said Bobby the bandit.

"Me neither," said Billy the bandit.

"Then allow me introduce myself. The name is Caden," he said with a graceful bow. "Maybe you have heard of me by the name of The Pirate with a Heart of Gold?"

Bobby and Billy both gasped, their wooden clubs dropping into the white sand below. Now they recognized Caden. They had seen drawings of him on posters around all the towns and villages they'd been to. They heard people telling tales of the brave and honorable pirate who fights against injustice and helps people in need. How whenever he is on a voyage he sails his red and black pirate flag. Billy and Bobby both looked out in the cove at the pirate ship anchored there. And sure enough, there it was, the red and black pirate flag hanging high on the mast.

"You see I am nothing like you or the other pirates out on the sea. I have chosen to use my strength and abilities to help others in need when no one else will. To protect the ones who need protecting. To make sure justice is served. That is how I live my life as a pirate on the open waters," Caden explained. "And furthermore, I don't need to steal. The people that I have helped though the years take care of me, everything from meals and lodging to clothes and ship repairs. We barter for services. And even if they don't have anything to offer at that time in exchange, I still help them. And do you know why? Because it is the right thing to do. It is just as simple as that."

Bobby and Billy just looked at Caden and thought how kindhearted he really was. How living an honest life must feel so good and bring so much joy to everyday life, knowing you are doing good deeds in the world.

Billy looked up at Bobby with tears in his eyes. "I don't want to be a bandit anymore, Bobby. I would rather live a good, honest life helping others rather than stealing from them," he said.

"You're not the only one Billy. I feel the same way too," said Bobby the bandit. "Oh Caden. I feel so ashamed of all the horrible things I have done in my life. Taking things that don't belong to me, bullying my way through life and hurting other people's feelings. Especially how that poor little cat was treated. He didn't deserve that. Is there anyway you could ever forgive me and help me to make right all the wrongs I have done?" asked Bobby the bandit.

"Yeah, me too, Caden. I feel the same way as my brother Bobby does," added Billy the bandit.

"To be honest with you both, I am going to need some time to talk this over with the rest of my crew. We make decisions as a group and if everyone agrees, then I will figure something out. But you will not go unpunished for your previous bad behaviors. And right now I need to take care of Fall and make sure he is all right. So I think the best thing right now is for you two to head back to your hideout and let me talk with my crew. I will come and find you once we have come to a decision," stated Caden.

"Oh thank you Caden," said Bobby and Billy. "We will go back to our hideout and wait for you for as long as it takes. We won't go anywhere. "

With that said, Bobby and Billy both reached down and picked up their wooden clubs off the beach. They turned around and headed back into the bushes making their way back to their secret hideout. Not knowing what would become of them, the two bandit brothers turned around one last time to wave goodbye.

Chapter Five

Fall Becomes an Official Pirate …

Caden called out to Mia and signaled to her that it was safe to come back to shore. As Mia approached the sandy beach, Caden waded into the cool seawater up to his knees. He held his hands out towards Mia so she could pass Fall over to him. But as soon as his hands reached out, Fall sprung through the air, into his arms and right up against his chest. Caden laughed and wrapped his arms around Fall, holding him tight. Fall just purred and purred. Caden smiled and felt the warmest feeling he has ever felt fill his heart. He knew from that moment on that he would forever protect Fall, no matter what the situation was, for as long as he lived.

"I need to take a closer look at you to make sure you are okay," Caden said to Fall.

Caden placed Fall on a nearby log to get a better look at him. Fall's fur had completely dried by this time and his eyes were sparkling in the sunshine. He didn't seem to be hurt anywhere and he definitely had a lot of energy.

"It looks like you are okay to me!" said Caden.

"I told you I was okay," Fall smiled. Then his expression went serious. "Caden? What is going to happen to the two bandits that took me away and locked me up in that cage?"

"Well Fall…that is up to you. What do you think we should do with them?" asked Caden.

Fall looked away and thought for a few moments. Turning back towards Caden he said, "I think they deserve a second chance. They seemed like they really wanted your help to change and become better people. Everyone makes mistakes sometimes…I know I have. And sometimes it is really hard to ask for forgiveness and help changing. So maybe they really do want to be better people and do good deeds in their lives."

Caden smiled. "I am really impressed with you, Fall. You are a very wise cat for being so young. And you have a warm heart as well. To be able to give those two bandits a second chance after what they had done to you, takes a lot of understanding, love and forgiveness. I can see you and I are going to get along very well together," said Caden. "Let's see what the rest of the crew thinks, okay?"

"Okay," said Fall.

So Caden called Mia, Gussy, Fin and Windy over to discuss what they should do with the bandits. After a long conversation, they came to an agreement. They all decided that they would give the two bandits a second chance. The bandits would have to prove themselves loyal and trustworthy by working as deckhands on the ship and returning all the treasures and supplies that they had stolen. If they managed to complete these tasks, they would be welcomed into Caden's crew.

"One more very important matter I'd like to discuss since everyone is all here," said Caden. "I would like to take this opportunity to appoint Fall as my second-in-command and make him an official pirate to our crew."

Fall's eyes widen with excitement. He couldn't believe what he was hearing. *Becoming the second-in-command to Caden and an official pirate?* This was surely the greatest honor Fall had ever been offered.

"I second that!" Mia stated.

"Me too!" said Windy.

"I do as well," stated Fin. "Well I guess that just leaves me to vote," said Gussy. He turned to ask Fall, "Do you feel you can serve dutifully as the second-in-command and an official pirate to this ship and its crew?"

"Yes Sir!" exclaimed Fall.

"Well then, I give my vote in favor of Fall becoming the second-in-command and an official pirate!" boasted Gussy. "You deserve it kid!"

Fall turned and looked up at Caden. "Caden, are you sure about this?" he asked.

"Of course I am sure. There is nothing I want more than to have you alongside of me on every one our journeys," said Caden.

"Then I accept this honor," stated Fall with a big smile on his face.

"There will still be room for me too, right Caden?" asked Gussy.

"Ah…Gussy, you know I could never replace you. You are like the ship's mascot. And everyone knows that any good pirate has to have a brave and trustworthy parrot by his side," laughed Caden.

Everyone was so excited and happy. Mia was cheering with Gussy. Windy and Fin both blew water from their blowholes and splashed around in the water. Caden looked down at Fall. He couldn't believe how this little cat had changed his life in a blink of an eye. Fall had given more meaning to his life now than he ever thought possible. Something in his heart told him to protect this little cat at all costs. He is truly something special.

"Ah, I almost forgot! Any new pirate needs a full pirate name!" stated Caden. "So, now that Fall is an officially a pirate, he needs a full pirate's name. Let's see here. What shall it be?" Caden said rubbing his chin. "Well, we definitely have to keep the first name as Fall. So what about the middle name? Any ideas?" Caden asked the crew.

"May I make a suggestion?" Mia asked.

"Yes please Mia," said Fall excitedly.

"When I was a young mermaid my best friend was a seahorse named Landon. He was my very best friend until the day we had to say goodbye. To this day, I miss him dearly and it would be an honor to have Fall carry on his name."

Fall was very touched by Mia's words.

"Landon..." said Caden. "What do you think Fall?"

"Landon sounds like a fine name," said Fall.

Mia smiled happily and a single tear of joy fell from her eyes.

"So now onto your last name. Fall, if I may, I would like to offer this name to you...the name is Sully," said Caden. "Sully was the first pirate to rescue me and take me under his wing. He was like a father to me. He taught me how to live an honest life and to always help others. And most importantly, to always be true to myself," Caden explained. "I feel it fitting to have you take his last name since it seems you as well have a heart full of forgiveness and love."

"Sully...I like it very much Caden," said Fall. "And I would be honored to carry that name with me."

"Fall Landon Sully...Yup, fits well together don't you think Fall?" asked Gussy.

"I think it's a fine name for a pirate Fall," Mia said smiling.

"I love it!" exclaimed Fall.

"Then that settles it. From this moment on, Fall will now be known as Pirate Fall Landon Sully!" announced Caden.

Everyone rejoiced and suddenly it felt more like a family now instead of a crew. Happiness and laughter filled the air.

"Now, one last thing left to do. And that is to have Fall take a pirate oath in front of witnesses," explained Caden.

"Fall, are you ready for the final step in becoming a true official pirate?" asked Caden.

"Yes Sir. I sure am," said Fall.

"What you have to do is take the Heart of Gold Pirate's Oath," said Caden.

"What is The Heart of Gold Pirate's Oath?" asked Fall.

"It is an oath you take, in front of witnesses, to live your life by and to follow with everything you have inside of you," explained Caden."

"I am ready," said Fall.

"Now you must repeat after me," said Caden. "I, Fall Landon Sully, promise to live my life honestly. To always help others that are in need of help, to always protect others that are in need of protecting and to never, ever harm an innocent life. I, Fall Landon Sully, am now and forever a pirate with a heart of gold."

Fall smiled his biggest smile ever. He repeated the oath, word for word. He was now and forever, officially, a pirate. Caden had never felt so proud. Everyone was cheering and splashing around. Caden picked up Fall and cuddled him in his arms. Fall nuzzled Caden's face and started purring. He knew in his heart that he would forever be by Caden's side for the rest of his life. No matter what obstacles came before him, he would stay loyal to Caden.

"So, Pirate Fall Landon Sully, looks like we are going to have to keep our eyes out for some pirate clothing for you," said Caden.

"Do I get a real pirate sword, too?" asked Fall.

"I don't know…what do you think Fin?" Caden asked.

"Well, Fall is an official pirate now so I don't see why not. But you must give him proper training," said Fin.

"I agree Fin. I will start training him tomorrow. But tonight we should have a huge feast to celebrate!" exclaimed Caden.

Gussy volunteered to handle the preparations for the feast himself. So he set out to collect all the bananas and melons he could find, as well as some coconuts and tropical fruits. He was going to make sure this feast would be a special one for Caden, Fall, and the rest of the crew. Gussy was so happy to see Caden smiling again. Gussy knew that as much as Fall needed Caden's help and friendship, Caden needed Fall's just the same.

Suddenly Caden remembered the bandit brothers. They were waiting for him at their hideout.

"Oh, I almost completely forgot about them," said Caden.

"Forgot about who Caden?" asked Fall.

"The bandit brothers. I told them to wait for me and I would come and speak with them once I knew what to do with them," explained Caden. "I guess I have some time before Gussy has the feast all ready. What do you say, Fall Landon Sully? Would you like to come with me to talk to those guys?"

Fall thought for a moment and then replied, "Yes, I will go with you. Being I am your second-in-command now," said Fall smiling.

Not too sure what would await them when they arrived at the hideout, or even if the bandits could be trusted, but this matter had to be dealt with and Caden felt he had to trust and follow Falls lead. So off they went. With a quick stop to tell Mia where they were headed and when they would be back, Fall and Caden disappeared into the bushes following a tiny path that was left by the bandits.

Chapter Six

The Secret Garden and the Golden Medallion…

It wasn't long before Caden and Fall came upon a little wooden house next to a crystal clear lagoon. And next to the little house was the waterfall that Fall had seen when he first arrived on the island. He couldn't believe how beautiful it was here. Huge palm trees lined the lagoon, some bearing bananas, some pineapples and others coconuts. And what amazing smells came from this area. The air smelled of sweet tropical flowers and fresh fruits. All these wonderful smells were making Fall hungry. He couldn't wait to get back to the feast and see what Gussy had in store for them. But first he knew that they had to deal with the bandit brothers.

Caden and Fall walked up the sandy pathway, which lead to the little wooden house. Upon reaching the front door, Caden grabbed the large cast iron ring and knocked three times. Caden stepped back and looked down at Fall.

"Now you stay close to me Fall. I want to be sure these two bandits really meant what they said earlier. I know you trust them but I have dealt with many people in my travels and sometimes people will lie and say anything to get out a sticky situation. So until I give the okay, you stick by my side, agreed?" asked Caden.

"Agreed," said Fall.

With still no answer from his previous knocking, Caden stepped back up to the front door and knocked three more times. He stepped back down again right next to Fall. Just then the front door creaked open and out popped Billy's head.

"Wow…you really came!" said Billy the bandit. "Hey Bobby, you will never believe who is here!"

Bobby came out from around the corner of the house, holding a gardening hoe in one hand and a rake in his other.

"Looks like you have decided what to do with us then," said Bobby the bandit.

Caden took Fall by the arm and pulled him in closer to him.

"I am here because Fall has decided to forgive you both and let you make amends. So the crew and I have all talked it over and decided to give you both a second chance. That is why we are here. So do you two still stand by your word to become honest and kindhearted people?" asked Caden.

"Absolutely Caden!" said Billy.

"We meant every word we said. We truly want to change our ways and we would be grateful for your help in doing so," stated Bobby.

Caden knew he had dealt with many men who have said the same thing to him before just to get out of punishment but something told him that these two meant what they were saying. And plus this would mean a lot to Fall as well. So he decided to trust these two and truly help them change their ways.

"All right then. You two better not screw this up because I will be watching you closely," said Caden. "It is not going to be easy work for either of you but it will be worth it in the end if you stick it out and prove to me and my crew that you both have honestly changed for the better."

"You can count on me Caden. I will show you. I will work as hard as I have to and earn your trust and respect." Bobby dropped down to his knees next to Fall, "And I want to say how very sorry I am for what Billy and I did to you, Fall. You didn't deserve to be taken from your home and treated like that. I am truly, very sorry." The tears ran down Bobby cheeks.

"Me too," said Billy, dropping to his knees. "I will make it up to you. I promise. I will be a good person from now on and make you proud. "

Caden looked down at Fall and smiled. He felt that the bandits were telling the truth, but only time could tell. He would try his best to work with these bandits since it meant so much to Fall.

"From now on you two are no longer know as bandits but as members of our crew and you will have to serve as deckhands on our ship," said Fall. "And another thing, you need to return all the stolen goods and supplies you have stolen. It doesn't matter how long it will take, you must return all that you can."

"That's right," said Caden. "I don't want one single piece of stolen treasure left behind. It all needs to go back to its rightful owners."

"That's no problem, Caden," said Bobby. "We pretty much have everything we have ever stolen stashed here. Plus, we still have a lot of the supplies left, too! I will make sure I get everything together and make a list of the people we stole from."

"Sounds good to me," said Fall. "But, can I ask you a question, Bobby?"

"Sure Fall, what is it?" said Bobby.

"Why are you carrying around a gardening hoe and rake on an sandy island?" Fall asked.

Bobby and Billy looked at each other and smiled. "Come with me. You will have to see it to believe it," said Bobby.

And with that Bobby turned and walked around the corner of the little wooden house, heading towards the backyard. Billy followed close behind and Caden walked alongside Fall. Arriving at the backyard Fall couldn't believe his eyes! There, before him, lay the most beautiful garden he had ever seen. Luscious berry bushes and tall fruit trees. All different kinds of vegetables were growing too! And an herb garden! There was a little fresh water pond with croaking frogs jumping about and tiny little hummingbirds darting from flower to flower. This was the coolest garden Fall had ever seen.

"This has got to be the coolest place I have ever seen," said Fall. "And you were right Bobby! I wouldn't have believed it if I hadn't seen it with my very own eyes. How did you get all these things to grow here on this sandy island?"

"Well, you see, every time we sailed out to a different port, we would search the land for the finest soil. And if we found some, we would fill up a few sacks with the soil to bring back here. So throughout the years we have built this garden, sack by sack, bringing new vegetation to the garden to grow. Now that it is as big as we would like it to be, we can focus on just growing all our favorite fruits and vegetables. This way we will always have fresh food to eat," explained Bobby.

"Yup," said Billy, "We like to stay healthy so all we eat is fresh fruits and vegetables. And this way we never worry about running out of food."

"Perfect! You both will be in charge of cooking all the meals on the ship then. Make sure we are stocked up with all fresh fruits and vegetables from your garden before we set out to sea," said Caden.

Caden looked down at Fall, gazing out over the garden. He felt it was okay to give Fall the go ahead to check out the garden. He could see the excitement in Fall's eyes and truly felt that Bobby and Billy posed no threat to him.

"Fall, would you like to take a look around and explore the garden?" asked Caden.

"Oh yes!" exclaimed Fall with excitement in his voice. He couldn't believe that these two brothers had created such a beautiful and relaxing place. It was so peaceful and calming.

"Bobby, is it okay if I look around?" asked Fall.

"Sure is. And feel free to enjoy any fruits and berries you like. Everything in this garden is delicious," said Bobby.

"Awesome! Thank you Bobby," said Fall.

So Fall took off down the path into the garden. He couldn't believe how many different varieties of plants were growing here. Everything smelled so good. There were some plants with leaves so big he could take a nap in one. Others were tiny little seedlings just beginning to grow. Fall continuing down the path to the little freshwater pond. The frogs there didn't even jump away from him when he approached them. They had the most amazing markings on their bodies. So bright and colorful. Fall reached down and picked up one to get a closer look at him.

"So you're the one the legend speaks of," said the frog.

"What are you talking about Mr. Frog? What legend?" asked Fall.

"You will know in time, young one. All in due time," said the frog. And with those last words the frog leapt from Fall's paw and into the pond, diving into the water and disappearing under a rock. *I wonder what that was all about. A legend? What kind of a legend? And what does it have to do with me?* Fall kept those thoughts in the back of his mind but for right now he wanted to explore as much of this magnificent garden that he could. It was just so amazing to be inside such a beautiful place. Fall kept on exploring all the new sights and smells. He was having so much fun discovering all the different areas of the garden. He lost count of how many colorful flowerbeds and sweet smelling plants he had found. There were just too many to keep track of!

Then something shimmering caught his eye. Fall headed down the path that led to the shoreline. Stepping onto the warm white sandy beach he could see the shiny object clearly now.

Sticking out from the sand just beneath the water's edge was a golden medallion. Fall reached down into the turquoise blue water and grabbed the medallion. Pulling it from the sand he noticed it had a twine rope tied to it. It was a necklace! A real gold medallion necklace! *Wow! I found my first piece of treasure!* He examined the medallion more closely and saw that carved into one side was an old pirate ship. The pirate ship was carved in such great detail that its beauty mesmerized Fall. Flipping the medallion over he noticed four initials carved into it. The initials were *CLCS*. Fall wondered what those initials stood for. *Possibly the name of the pirate ship? Or maybe the owner's initials of this medallion?* Whatever the initials meant Fall just knew they were important. For some reason he felt he was meant to find this medallion.

Knowing that he had been gone for sometime now, Fall began making his way back up the beach and through the garden path. He couldn't help but think about what the frog said about him being the one the legend spoke of. *But what did that mean? And what legend?* Fall just had to know what that frog meant by telling him that. So he headed straight over to the pond and tried calling out to the frog.

"Mr. Frog…? Mr. Frog…? Are you still here? Please, Mr. Frog, please explain to me what you meant when you said I was the one the legend spoke of," Fall pleaded.

But no reply came. Not even a glimpse of the frog that he spoke with earlier. Fall knew he had been gone for too long now and didn't want Caden worrying about him. So he had no other choice but to continue to make his way back through the garden towards the little wooden house. Holding the medallion in his paw he tried to think of what the frog was trying to tell him. *But why didn't he just tell me when we were talking? Maybe he didn't know anything else or maybe he wasn't supposed to even tell me.* Too many thoughts and questions filled Fall's head. All he knew was that he couldn't wait to show Caden what he had found. Caden would surely be proud of him for finding his first piece of pirate treasure! And what better than finding a beautiful golden medallion on his first day as a pirate?

Chapter Seven

The Legend of the Golden Medallion...

Fall had finally made it back to the little wooden house. Upon arriving he could see that Caden, Bobby, and Billy were just finishing loading up all the sacks that were filled with the fruits and vegetables they would need for their next voyage. Hurrying over to Caden in excitement to show him his newly found treasure, Fall tripped and fell in the sand. His golden medallion went flying through the air and landed at Caden's feet. Caden reached down and picked up the medallion. He brushed the sand off it and took a closer look. To his surprise he recognized it right away! It was the golden medallion that belonged to Sully, the pirate that took him in when he was a young boy and was like a father to him. Caden hurried over to Fall and helped him up from the ground, gently brushing the sand off Fall's fur.

"Fall, are you alright?" asked Caden.

"Yeah, I just got too excited and wasn't paying attention to what was in my path," explained Fall. He looked down at the sand and saw the large stick he tripped over. Kicking it out of the path and into the bushes he then turned to Caden and said, "I wanted to show you what I found! It's a gold meda…."

"Medallion," Caden finished Fall's sentence. "A gold medallion. Fall, where did you find this?" asked Caden.

"Down on the shoreline just past the garden. Why Caden?" asked Fall.

"Fall, this medallion used to belong to Sully. Captain Liam Caden Sully. The pirate that rescued me when I was a young boy," explained Caden. "That is also how I got my name. He gave me his middle name and raised me as if I were his own son."

Fall could see tears beginning to fill Caden's eyes. Caden quickly wiped the tears away and handed the medallion back to Fall.

"This must be some sort of sign that you and I were meant to meet each other Fall," said Caden. "I am happy that you found Sully's medallion and now I believe it belongs to you."

"Caden, before I found the medallion I met a frog that told me I was the one the legend spoke of and I would know more all in due time," explained Fall. "Before I could ask him any other questions he disappeared into the pond. Not long after I found this golden medallion. I went back to the pond to try and find the frog again and ask him more questions but he never came out. What do you think he meant Caden?" asked Fall.

"Fall, I'm sorry. I really have no idea what he was talking about but I think I know someone who will. But first let's ask Bobby and Billy since you did find it on their beach," said Caden.

"I agree Caden. After all it is the right thing to do," said Fall.

Caden smiled, picked up Fall and gave him a long gentle hug. He knew that for some reason or another he was meant to rescue this little cat and protect him with his life from this day forward. He wasn't sure what the frog was talking about and Sully had never told him of a legend but if anyone were to know about a legend it would be the one that was by Sully's side at all times, Gussy. But first Caden wanted to see if Bobby or Billy knew anything about the medallion and how it ended up on their island.

"Well now, let's find Bobby and Billy and see if they know anything about the medallion being on their island," Caden said as he placed Fall back on the sand.

"Absolutely," said Fall. "But first can you please tie the medallion around my neck for me, Caden? I want to wear it to our feast!"

"I sure can," said Caden.

So Caden leaned down and tied the golden medallion around Fall's neck. Just as the medallion touched Fall's chest Caden noticed a slight glow or glimmer to the medallion. It seemed to become apart of Fall as soon as it was placed on him. Caden needed answers and he needed them now.

"We better get moving, Fall. Gussy is probably all ready to start the feast and everyone is waiting for us to return," said Caden. "And we still need to talk to Bobby and Billy and ask them about this medallion. They are all packed and ready to come with us so we can ask them at the feast. How does that sound Fall?" asked Caden.

"Sounds good to me, Caden!" Fall agreed.

So back through the path leading to the other side of the island went Fall and Caden. Caden was anxious to speak with Gussy in regards to the golden medallion, but he needed to ask Bobby and Billy first. So he picked up his pace and Fall followed right behind him.

Upon reaching the other side of the island they could see the feast was all set up by the water's edge. How beautiful and festive everything looked. Gussy really outdid himself with all the fruits, nuts, and berries. As well as making a special blend of fruit juice from melons and pineapples. He had laid out huge plantation leaves on the sand to use as seating mats and beautiful tropical flowers were spread about the shoreline in an array of colors. Split coconuts were used for juice cups and Bobby and Billy had created a small bonfire close enough to the shore for everyone to gather around.

Mia came swimming up to the shoreline with Fin and Windy.

"All right, now that Caden and Fall have returned we can begin the celebration feast!" Mia exclaimed.

"Then let's get to it!" said Gussy. "But first I have a little surprise for Fall. Remember this little guy?" Gussy asked Fall.

Out from behind a tree popped the young monkey that Fall met the first night he was on the island. The young monkey that gave him the banana and melon.

"Of course I do!" exclaimed Fall excitedly. "I am so happy you could make it to our feast. And thanks again for the banana and melon."

"No worries Fall. I am just glad you finally got out of that horrible cage. And I see that the bandits have turned over a new leaf as well," said the young monkey.

"They sure have. They will be working as deckhands on our ship until they prove themselves loyal and trustworthy. Might take some time but I am sure they can do it," expressed Fall. "By the way, I never got your name."

"The name's Milo," said the young monkey.

"That's a cool name," Fall said. "Milo the monkey. Suits you well Milo!"

Everyone seemed to be enjoying themselves. Laughing at jokes that Fin was telling. Savoring all the wonderful food and drinks that Gussy had gathered with the help of Milo. Windy and Mia were sitting on the waters edge eating strawberries and grapes together. Bobby and Billy were down next to the bonfire, enjoying the company of their new crew. Caden and Fall walked over to the bonfire and sat down near Bobby and Billy.

"I want to ask you both something and I want nothing but the truth from you two. Do you understand?" Caden asked Bobby and Billy.

"Of course Caden. After what you have done for us, giving us a second chance, we wouldn't dare cross you," said Bobby.

"I wouldn't dare cross you either Caden," said Billy.

"Do you know anything about a golden medallion with a pirate ship carved into one side and the initials *CLCS* carved into the other side?" asked Caden.

Bobby and Billy both looked at each other with confused looks on their faces. They genuinely seemed not to know what Caden was talking about.

"I have never seen a gold medallion like that before in my life Caden. And trust me, I would remember something like that," stated Bobby.

"Neither have I Caden, honest," said Billy.

Caden has dealt with enough liars and thieves to know when one is telling the truth and when one is lying, and these two really didn't seem to know anything about the medallion.

"Well then, there should be no dispute if Fall were to claim ownership to this medallion we speak of, correct?" asked Caden, knowing full well that he had every right to the ownership of the medallion but wished to gift it to Fall.

"Absolutely no dispute Caden. If Fall found it then by all means it is his to keep," said Bobby.

"I agree with Bobby," said Billy. "Fall has just found his very first piece of treasure! Here's to Fall and his first treasure find as a pirate!" Billy held up his coconut and toasted Fall. Everyone raised their coconuts and drank a sip of fruit nectar to honor Fall.

Gussy flew over and landed on Caden's shoulder.

"So what's this I hear of Fall and his first treasure find?" asked Gussy.

"Here Gussy! Take a look! I found it on the other side of the island just on the shoreline. Isn't it amazing?" Fall grabbed the medallion and held it up so Gussy could take a closer look. Gussy's eye widened and he turned to Caden.

"Caden, don't you know what this is?" asked Gussy.

"Of course I know Gussy. It belonged to Sully. I am just amazed that after all this time Fall ends up finding it, by chance, on the shore of island owned by "former" bandits," explained Caden.

"Oh Caden," said Gussy. "You must not know the true meaning behind finding this medallion: The Legend of Captain Sully's Golden Medallion."

"Yes Gussy! A frog told me I was the one the legend spoke of and I would know more in due time. Do you know what he meant by that?" asked Fall.

"I sure do Fall. Legend goes that the one who finds the medallion is the one meant to find Captain Sully. And of course you know what Sully had with him at all times don't you?" asked Gussy.

"You?" joked Caden.

"Besides me, Sully always kept with him the treasure map of the infamous lost land of PaiPohm," explained Gussy

"What are you talking about Gussy?" asked Caden.

"Legend states that Captain Sully had a curse put on the medallion, but not just any curse, a curse of good instead of evil. One that will lead a worthy, loyal and true pirate to find him if he was ever to be lost at sea," explained Gussy. "But that one would first have to find the medallion in order for the good curse to be awakened and begin its magic. Now that Fall has found the medallion, it is only time we wait upon to see if the legend is true or not."

"Gussy, you know that Sully was lost at sea," Caden said sadly. "You and I were the only ones who survived the shipwreck. After that we searched days, weeks and even months with no signs of him. We searched various islands, ports, and even went up rivers and still never found one clue that he was still alive. How could this possibly be true?" asked Caden.

"If the legend is true, the medallion will let off a faint glow or glimmer once it is placed around the neck of a worth, loyal and true pirate. Only then will it come to life. And once the medallion has come to life it will begin to glow and glimmer stronger the closer you get to finding Sully…or so the legend goes," explained Gussy.

"The medallion has already began to glow. I have seen it with my own eyes as I tied it around Fall's neck. I swear I have seen it with my own eyes. It must be alive now!" exclaimed Caden.

"It's true. As soon as I picked it up from the sand it began to glow a little bit. I thought it was just the way the sun was hitting it but now it all makes sense. Plus what the frog told me," explained Fall.

Gussy, Caden and Fall all looked at one another. Excitement filled each of their hearts with the possibility of finding Captain Sully. Fall could see that Caden's eyes began to tear up a bit, so he hurried over to him and jumped in his lap.

"Don't cry Caden. I will do everything I can to find Captain Sully. I can promise you that. I will not give up. I will spend the rest of my life in search for him if that's what it takes. It is the very least I can do after everything you have done for me," expressed Fall.

Caden looked down at Fall and gave him a little kiss on the top of his head. How lucky he was to have crossed paths with this little cat. A tiny little creature that in such a short period of time has brought life back into him and a warmth in his heart he thought he would never feel again.

Caden stood to his feet and addressed his whole crew, "Well then, looks like we have our next voyage set out for us! We will set sail at dawn in search for Captain Liam Caden Sully!" exclaimed Caden.

And with that, everyone rejoiced. The thought of possibly finding Captain Sully made everyone extremely happy.

Caden walked over and sat down next to Fall. Handing him a coconut cup, he poured some fruit nectar into it.

"This is just the beginning, kid. You and I are going to do a lot of good things together. I can just feel it," said Caden, raising his cup to Fall.

"I know what you mean," said Fall, raising his cup to Caden. "I have the same feeling."

"Well it looks like I have two pirates to keep an eye on now," said Gussy. "I guess now I'll have my wings full."

"Oh Gussy. We are not that bad to watch over. We won't be too much trouble for you," said Caden.

"Yeah, don't worry Gussy. I will be on my best behavior. Since now I am a second-in-command pirate!" said Fall.

"So what do we do next, Caden?" Fall asked, looking up at Caden.

"Well Fall, all we need to do now is set sail, follow the signs of that medallion and let it take us to our destination. And hopefully, just hopefully we will find Sully there," Caden said looking out towards the horizon.

Fall held onto Caden's words. Looking out over the ocean Fall couldn't help but think about how his life has changed so much in such a short period of time. How he had met so many new friends, became a second-in-command pirate, and found a loving friend like Caden to be by his side. Fall truly felt like the luckiest cat in the world and he knew that this was just the beginning of their lifelong journey together. And so their first adventure would begin…the search for Captain Liam Caden Sully and the lost land of PaiPohm!

The End

Made in the USA
Monee, IL
05 November 2022

17137848R00038